If I Go Missing

poems

Carol Lynne Knight

With an introduction by Diane Wakoski

Fernwood
PRESS

If I Go Missing

Poems

©2022 by Carol Lynne Knight

Fernwood Press
Newberg, Oregon
www.fernwoodpress.com

Printed in the United States of America

Cover and page design: Mareesa Fawver Moss

Cover art: "Spring Thaw, Colorado," digital painting
by Carol Lynne Knight (carollynneknight.com)

Author photo: Becki Rutta (beckirutta.com)

ISBN 978-1-59498-084-8

Contents

Three

Four

Five

Epilogue

Introduction

The poems in *If I Go Missing* contain the complex, haunting voice of a woman who may lose herself when she admits passionate love for a man into her life. The thrilling, powerful poems detailing her failed marriage to a city cop are the grounding for a lifelong concern with what it means to "go missing."

Her clever romance with television detectives is a trope I've never seen used in poetry. As she persistently asks Wallander, Columbo, Inspector Morse, Luther, Jane Tennison, even Sherlock Holmes, to search for her if she goes missing, she can speculate on the many ways the dread of disappearing can overshadow a woman's life. Knight has turned this wonderful and engaging trope of the television detective into some memorable and, really, life saving observations — in the closing poem, "Just Rising," she offers "fierce opposition" to giving in, to becoming invisible.

Knight's images of beautiful objects to be found in her world, even catalogues of them, are varied and mysterious in each poem. In fact, catalogues are a dominant feature of many of Knight's poems — not necessarily long and always relevant, they often lead to revelations about who she really is, not where she is.

In "The Ex," she eloquently admits if she went missing, her ex-husband could find her.

> All those broken locks, those open windows —
> he will investigate every one with the stubborn
> authority of an ex-cop, searching for
> that one true thing that defines me.

Yet, throughout the book, the fear that she might never be found is not assuaged. In "Abandoned Car Park," we are told not to call the French detective Eddie Caplan to find her as the bodies of the hapless victims he tries to rescue continue to stack up. Many-layered and colorful, these poems are extremely controlled. The irony is that the figure behind these explorations could never go missing. She is unforgettable.

— Diane Wakoski

January 2020

Acknowledgments

My thanks to the editors of the following publications where these poems first appeared, sometimes in a slightly different form:

Broome Review: "There is No Waiting"

Dime Show Review: "Porch Rail"

Drowning Gull: "State Line" and "Fast Cars"

J: "What He Brought Home"

Louisiana Literature: "Mowing," "Riding Shotgun," and "Target"

Postcard Poems and Prose Magazine: "Serpentine" and "Hollow Point"

Slink Chunk Press: "What Smooth Object," "Passport Expired," "Bottle Blonde," "The Ex," and "Russian Accent"

Slipstream: "Brass"

www.poetz.com: "Brass"

Anthologies:

Off the Cuffs (Soft Skull Press): "The Wall"

While the act of writing is mostly solitary, the act of poetry wants a community — I am so thankful to my community of writers and lovers of poetry, who over the years have provided audience, comment, inspiration, and encouragement. In this community, I count my beloved Java Girls (Mary Jane Ryals, Melanie Rawls and Donna Decker), my Anhinga Press cohorts, Kristine Snodgrass and former co-director, Rick Campbell, who introduced me to a whole new world when I began designing and editing for the press. I send my thanks all over the country to the Anhinga poets I have worked with to design, edit, and publish their books for the privilege of diving so deep into their words. My thanks to the Tallahassee community, who listen to, share, and applaud poetry — sometimes my own.

And, thank you to my friends and family, who combed these pages at the proofing stage: Donna Decker, Melanie Rawls, Mary Jane Ryals, Rob Knight, and Shannon McEwen Knight.

My thanks to the Hambidge Center for the Arts and the Bowden House, where many of these poems were written, for their offer of solitude and support.

For their generous comments, my thanks to Erika Meitner and Chad Sweeney.

A special thanks to Diane Wakoski for her introduction. Her book, *Medea the Sorceress,* was a revelation to me and helped me toward a more expansive way to write and take on the world.

Thank you to John Sibley Williams for his expertise, and for finding a good home for *If I Go Missing.* To Eric Muhr and Mareesa Fawver Moss, at Fernwood Press, my deepest thanks for sending this book into the world.

Small Blue Eggs

— Wallander

If I go missing,
send Kurt Wallander
to find me. He can cypher
my icy subtitles still fingered
on the bathroom mirror.

His thumb will stroke
the objects I leave behind
like small blue eggs, robin sized.

He will unwrap tissue from
the delicate snake bones
we found in the juniper woods,
and finger the limestone rock,
retrieved for a kiss
from the bottom
of Half Moon Lake —
all my childish things.

He will open the lacquered box
that holds spare keys,
inspect a fragment
of driftwood stolen
from the river's mouth.

If I go missing,
he will glimpse
the horizon folding
into the dunes,
the sandpipers dithering
in the strand,
and know that
I would flee.

One

State Line

The exit signs read Pensacola Bay. At Dairy Queen, the server creates a tower of vanilla that cants to the left — waiting for my tongue to even out its creamy architecture. Driving one-handed, cone finished, napkins tossed, I am still sticky, but caught in the road's momentum — I lick my fingers clean in Alabama.

Crossing the Mississippi-Louisiana line: under I-10, the Pearl River is a brown slither thru green marshes quilting the landscape for miles. I imagine traveling the bridge to Malmö, lost in the inept conversation of Saga Norén, as she struggles to read my face. But, I have not flown to Denmark, only added a Swedish accent to my inner dialogue. Like driving over the state line, discontent is marked with signs, but invisible from the sky.

for salt

for moon hunger
a cleft of tides

that moment
when the
current shifts
from pushing
toward shore
to luring
us into the
far horizon

we are brine
evidence of stars
offered relentlessly
to a sun
mirrored
in the shoals

Fast Cars

I am still lost, Charlie Crews —
and although we drive fast cars,
somehow speed was not enough to bring us together.

I would stuff my Corvette with grocery bags,
my son's legs dangling over the rough
brown paper, the moment for speed abandoned,
the car, a beautiful beast asleep in the parking lot.

When you find me, we will share a moment
like small fish swimming together in the same bowl:
all could be shattered and we would still have that moment.

These cars, attachments we should abandon —
but if I am letting go, is it Zen to expect
that someone will catch me,
that there can be the repose of a cat
sleeping with curled paws and back legs splayed,
or must I release that reckless hope?

I will wait just 15 more minutes,
bargaining with my wristwatch.
Find me! I am dozing in the parking lot
at Burger King near the 49th Street overpass.
I thought I was waiting for my lover
but I don't think he ever loved me,
which made the minutes fry, then salt,
which made me imagine French fries
and a banyan tree spreading
its canopy over the asphalt.

We may have been condemned,
but now we can drive fast cars
and stop waiting for stalled lovers.
So, find me.
No one has taken me,
no one has hidden me,
but I am missing something.

If I am the girl waiting in the parking lot,
I shall bring a book, so I will not be waiting, but reading,
not listening for the rumbling muffler that signifies my lover,
whom I thought I loved, but as I remember him . . . could not now love,
except in that universal way that humans love their species.
(sigh!) — loving 7 billion people, a glorious exhaustion.

Find me Charlie Crews,
find the minute that is ours,
that fictional minute that is now,
but has passed since I asked you.

I am caught in the nanosecond
when my car keys disappear,
when I search everywhere — under, over,
inside every closet, purse, and drawer.
If I locate the keys, we can go on a road trip —
there is something easy
about conversation at 70 mph,
speech merged with speed, with confession,
with landscape and wind —
intercept me at the rest stop
on I-75 north of Paynes Prairie.
I'll be waiting, head against
the glass, book open.

Porch Rail

— Luther

If I am accused, perhaps guilty —
send DCI John Luther to find me.

I have escaped like a cat
balancing on the porch rail,
threading thru the bayside grass,
unkempt, almost wild, slipping into the water
beneath the mullet fisher's net.

The sun — a quiet lemon squeezing
over the long, low bridge to my island.
I am prey, like the mourning dove,
nesting under clacking palmetto fronds,
quietly jittering thru the sedge.
Follow me across the bay,
thru the tidal marshes, into the open Gulf.
Become a sting ray, become my shark.
We will consume the freedom
escape offers, and then rescinds.

Follow me into rough waters —
no longer suffer the confusions
of deceitful living — for we all are guilty,
all accused, all victims of the urban landslide —
watching others fall as if we pushed them,
pushing them as if they will fall and keep falling
while we peer over the rail, sweating, losing grace.

When he finds me, I will be floating
under the sky's slate pallor —
bay swallowing the weathered, listing docks,
the lights on the bridge smudged with fog,
the sough of calm seas, knived
with white caps, cleaved by rain.

Scrap of Crimson

— *True Detective, Season 1*

If I tear my dress and leave a scrap of crimson,
if I float like smoke rings above my imagined self,
Rust Cohle will find a pattern in the levitation,
pace off the evidence foot by foot,
sketch my ruptured life into his ledger.

At three, I was fearless — popped the hook
on the screen door with a broom stick
while my mother slept — and walked
alone toward Great Traverse Bay; pried open
the mouth of the neighbor's surly dog,
and peered inside — and always,
talk talk talking to everyone.

Find me fearless, again —
wake that kiss-anyone,
ride-on-the-back-of-a-motorcycle,
leaning-into-the-curves woman
curling under my bed. Find me resolute,
basking in atmospheric pleasures.

Search in your memory of a city —
caves of cement and PVC,
conduit stripped of copper,
insulation weeping from the ceilings,
an empty-warehouse-heart-beat echo
humming in the tires
as his peculiar cadence
drawls across the levee.
Out loud, we brood about black holes
and the mysteries of singularity,
the insect souls that ghost-sing in the swale.

We all have our betrayals —
rain pounding the windshield,
white fist on the road,
a swirl of skirt, last tango
of asphalt, dirt flying —
the sapphire sky held hostage.
Discover me lost, charmed
by the center yellow line,
intoxicated with too many headlights —
the road has become my addiction.

I leave tiny artifacts for the record —
an opal earring dangling
from the outstretched arm of a water oak,
a tatter of polyester leopard skin
snagged in the hinge of a rusty trailer door,
a penny crushed on the railroad track,
a derailed train, every cell in crisis,
wreckage, maybe redemption.

What Smooth Object

— The Bridge / Broen / Bron

Saga Norén would find me —
ask all the embarrassing questions,
in her blunt, autistic fashion.
She would spare none of my friends,
and quote the statistics that fringe
my life like a vintage feathered hat:
my chance of remarrying
lower than being struck by lightning,
my cancer recurrence wavering at 5 percent,
my burglar alarm that only deters amateurs.

She steps beyond the barricade
of regulations, that book she worships —
if she ever worships — all evidence sacred
and necessary, every clue to my disordered
existence leading nowhere,
but she threads them together to find me.

And if I ask her,
What led you across
the Oresund Bridge?
What smooth object gave you the scent
of my imperfect life? I was sleeping under the bridge,
its cables singing, the moon breathing
into my tattered shawl, my forsaken dress —
waiting to be found.

When I ask, she turns back to the bridge,
its impossible sighs.

Suitcases

If I go in winter, I will leave
frost cursives on the glass,
scripting things I do not know.
It is a kind of love, revealing what
is hidden, only to you —
how my folding skin catches anguish
and tree branches divide
the twilight into a sunless mosaic,
how I am breathless on the stairs
and suddenly remember
a kind of rape, like it was
yesterday, and am so sickened,
I stop writing that sentence.

How you shall know everything —
even whispers from the seat
behind me on the plane
that become my secrets
as we walk down the concourse,
fetch our suitcases, and find our sons
waiting in the low, vibrating
cave of the car park,
how they lift our bags,
stow them in the trunk,
and then offer a solid embrace.
That secret — I should tell it now,
but it has become wordless.

It is my sacrament,
the memory that is not memory
until it is told to the next.
When I am gone, will you remember
as you pack my secrets like old clothes,
will you lift my favorite blouse
and breathe its scent — that one true thing?

Two

We Don't Know How to Swim

A soldier arrives for dinner every night. Add radio squawk to the
cuisine. Violence sits down and prays for calm. I serve it with
overbaked casserole — look up and the ceiling undulates as we
eat, look down and our feet seem to float over the rug. We are
not drowning, but we don't know how to swim.

We fret about the unrest and chaos churning where he patrols — the
Marielitos camping in our high school stadium, crowding the
stands we used to crowd — a different sea of humanity — more
needy, more lost and volatile.

Riots change everything. There is burning, there is fear, there is
despair dusted with ash, a news hour desperation at the dinner
table. Now — we are drowning.

burr

and sticker
rose stems
and barbed wire
fencing beauty

sand spurs on cuffs
splinter and blood
tiny pain
small poke

catfish whiskers
poison spikes
bee sting
and venom
slithering
from a nightmare

fear is bondage,
life has fangs.

Brass

He showers and sings the green green grass of home
while I spread his uncreased just-off-the-hanger shirt
before me like an apron and piece by piece transfer brass
from the sweaty shirt I found on the closet floor.

The shower door slides open, warm moist air infiltrates the room.
I fasten a brass button to each front pocket, initials and wings
to the collar point, center the name plate over the right pocket,
badge over the left, long pin thru bound holes, then poked
thru cardboard to keep it straight.

He shaves — the razor comforts me, stroking his skin like cat's tongue.
I feel the shift of intimacy as my fingers pull his wallet, keys, loose change,
loose bullets, ragged rolaids, and scraps of license numbers,
tag numbers, phone numbers, zone numbers from his pockets.

Short bursts from the faucet rinse his razor, white foam pauses
in the drain. I adjust the velcro straps on his bulletproof vest,
slide the Kevlar panels into washed blue covers,
lay out clean underwear and socks.

I hear a slap of aftershave, snap of patent leather, chink of change,
his key in the lock as he leaves, and an unspoken lingering that
turns in the bed while stars fall to the floor beside me.

The Wall

The distant wail of sirens spills into my dreams.

You pull a twisted woman from the wreckage.
She is screaming. You find her baby —
a pale bundle of yellow
strangely flat on the asphalt.

At 2 a.m.
the paperwork is done,
the mother sedated,
the baby at the morgue.

While I sleep, fingers curled in the edge of a blanket,

you shed your uniform shirt
and gunbelt, stash them in the trunk
and head for the Boots and Saddle Bar;
to be washed in thick blue smoke
and the harp-sad sound of a juke box.

Other men in white T-shirts, shiny black lace-ups,
and almost-black blue pants straddle bar stools,
or lean into the wall and drink beer from cloudy glasses.
You tell the joke about the lawyer and the alligator.
Everyone laughs and no one

mentions babies, not even their own
at home asleep, where they will go
when last call echoes thru
the neon funk, and they must leave.

In the parking lot, the beat of rain has flatlined
and left a glistening silence between the cars.

Mowing

I wake you early — 2 p.m.
This is the day to mow the grass
before it gets so high we need a scythe
to cut it down. It is Miami May —
sun high, inland breeze sly and low.

You roll over, covering your head.
I croon your mother's old Saturday morning reveille,
Listen to the green grass grow!
You hate that song. It gets the rise I want
and your morning coffee, two sugars, lots of cream
gets you rolling. Soon the mower is cranked
and clipping thru the fat St. Augustine shoots,
flinging them on the sidewalk
for me to sweep up behind you.

You are a man who sweats
in an air-conditioned house,
stretched out on your recliner —
today, in this 90 percent humidity,
your T-shirt soon soaks thru.
Red-faced, and except for the geometric precision
of the swaths you cut, side by side across the lawn,
you are not enjoying this at all.
It's, *Shit!* when blades hit a rock,
Fuck! when the mower sputters to a halt,
and *Damn!* when the cool shower finally hits your back,
washing away the grit and sweat in time for supper.

When you leave for the station at 9 p.m.,
you say the yard work has worn you out,
you hope the bad guys stay home tonight.

They don't.

The 11 o'clock news shows overturned cars,
burning warehouses, exploding streetlights —

while we were working in the yard,
a Tampa jury acquitted four Miami police officers
of the death of Arthur McDuffie.*

Thirty-six hours later, you return
from what they now call the War Zone.

Next time, while the new yard service
mows the grass, I leave you sleeping
in the curtained twilight of our bedroom.

*Arthur McDuffie: a Black motorcyclist beaten by police
after a high-speed chase in Miami, 1979.*

Training Film

SCENE 1
Two officers parked outside the House of Pets — a boa constrictor
curls in the fluorescent twilight of the window, you tell the joke
about God and the lawyer who can't swim.

SCENE 2
At the corner, a black Camaro slips thru the red light,
hauls ass down 79th Street, jumps the curb, and shatters
the Gooney Golf dinosaur during your punchline.

SCENE 3
The driver of the Camaro fumbles for his license as you
step over the dinosaur, fold into your patrol car, radio for
a wrecker, and repeat the punchline — without looking back.

SCENE 4
Gunshots crack the air — a balloon of red goop splatters
across the Plexiglas cage behind your headrest.
It's bad timing, but the crew laughs anyway.

EPILOGUE
Flanked by uniforms at the premiere,
I recall the unsure surrender of pretending
to die, only to miss the punchline.

What He Brought Home

Uniforms from the dry cleaner on wire hangers
Cleat marks on his leg (from a crazed woman wearing golf shoes)
Bruises from a man armed with a broom (on angel dust)
A bomb threat
Stray cat women
Groupie waitresses
Drunken buddies
A sweaty, bullet-proof vest cover
A former Hells Angel named Froggy
A ten-day suspension
A shattered eardrum
A concussion and migraines
(when his patrol car was rear ended)
A lawsuit for one million dollars in punitive damages
A sleazy detective named Skip
An 80-pound dog that ate the garbage can
His girlfriend's cat
A 1948 Ford
A 1975 Corvette
A trophy for police-combat target shooting
His girlfriend's snub nosed .38
A .45 chrome automatic
A Teflon-coated .357 magnum
A .22 pistol
Empty bullet casings
A Holy Roller desk sergeant
A torn uniform shirt from the riots
A stained shirt from the Republican convention
War stories and lawyer jokes
Valium and hangovers
My last-chance cat from the vet
that he refused to put down —
who lived six more years.

There is No Waiting

for the wind to thrust
branches against the window.

It just comes
on the midnight shift, leaves
a silence shaped by rending fingers.

And there is no waiting for a hand to pull
black elastic tight across the face of a brass badge;
for his pay-phone voice to let you know
that he is not in the body bag they panned
so slowly on the evening news.
No waiting to receive a flag
if you sit in a metal folding chair
on fresh dirt draped with Astroturf.

It just happens after the AC hum drowns out
the number six bus at the corner every twenty minutes
and lawyers negotiate truth in narrow hallways,
but can't erase the headlines when
his accidental shooting is front-page news.
It comes when a TV news crew turns off their lights
and lets your shadows fall closer to the floor.

It just happens when you hear that sigh
as his dinner plate slides only four inches from the edge
of the table and his shoulders fall forward
enough to let you know — there is no waiting
for the devil to follow you home.

Three

Hollow Point

A king-size bed, a chrome .45 automatic loaded with hollow point
  rounds, reclining under empty pillows, a fan droning over cat
  prance and street threat. A woman who sleeps or doesn't —
  waiting for another midnight shift to end.

She dreams of the Everglades, targets tacked on scrub pine,
  the startling flash and kick. She dreams of glass breaking
  downstairs. She dreams her index finger is ice, melting fast.

When he comes home, there is talk to quash the dreams.

There is potential explosion. There is heat.

small fingernails

of transcendence
clipped ripped chewed
scattered to be collected
and analyzed for passion
and intent

touch being
difficult to fake
whether an earthquake
or flutter of finch wing

a body remembers
the scratch
slap caress
of fingers

the stroke
of a nail
small scribe
of temptation

Time Out

Back then, when we first married,
I didn't understand the nature of the game,
how the referee's whistle
was a safe, sweet sound,
how a coin toss decided
who would look into the sun,
throw against the wind,
how it all happened in an open field,
with clearly marked goals,
and all the players wore matching uniforms
and names across their chests.
When it was over, we would know
who won, who lost.
It was precise, ordered,
and brutal choreography.

These players are fallible, but they still survive,
even if there is rain and mud, snow or blistering sun.
Rest comes at set intervals. If you get confused,
you can call time out, and everyone stops
while you think about what to do,
catch your breath, pray a little.

Back then, I thought that fifteen minutes
could last as long as we needed,
that you would watch until your shift
began at midnight, when you would leave —
armed, brass polished, Kevlar vest
heavy under your shirt, ready
for the chaos of tripped alarms, weaving
drunks, beaten wives, and teenage pranks.

I yawned at the roar of the crowd.
First downs seemed endless,
and boring — not the chance
to start over, to finally get it right.
Back then, I called time-out
and walked in front of the television —
nude — before halftime.

Target

We park the truck behind a phalanx
of Australian pine that cuts across the Everglades
and tack up paper targets. My husband
hands me his polished .45 automatic.
The crack of practice ammo interrupts
a rhythmic hum and hiss singing in the sawgrass.

> I'm Annie Oakley, the cowgirl queen.
> My draw is quick and deadly.

Dark silhouettes of men expire
in a yellow haze falling thru the pines.
I'm in the groove — line up the sights,
squeeze without breathing until
the bullet rips into the twilight.

> I'm Annie Oakley and the bad guys
> are dropping like flies.

If I sleep with a gun under my pillow,
I must know how to aim for the heart.
It's a simple dance for eye and hand —
without flinching when you squeeze the trigger,
without anticipating the kick-pop discharge from the gun.

> I'm Annie Oakley,
> so reach for the sky.

My paper targets are tattered souls, drifting
toward Miami. I prop up milk cartons
for the final assault while my husband
reloads the gun. He jokes as he slides in the clip.
I aim for the spots on the cow and squeeze the trigger.

> I'm Annie Oakley.
> The crowd is on its feet.

I squeeze again — the air explodes.
My hands hang on as the gun kicks up over my head.
Tiny flames flash in my face. A hollow point bullet, designed
to shred flesh on impact, tears into the Everglades.
I lay down the gun and walk to the truck.

> I'm Annie Oakley.
> Don't play with me.

Riding Shotgun

My mattress purrs, the cat
amazed and flat, chases sleep across
a floral terrain. An ardor of rain
assaults the window, glazing streets
with reflections and skids.

Cat tail flicks back and forth
back and forth, windshield fogs,
wipers slap, our shower door shatters —
chunks of safety glass litter the intersection,
gasoline spills from the car like aftershave,
covers the bathroom counter, runs into the gutter.
Shampoo foams the crosswalk
before my hair ignites. The blanket
is soaked with sweat, with rain, with blood
from the body in the intersection.

From the closet, sirens wail behind your uniforms.
A high-speed chase careens thru umbrellas and off-ramps,
twists around hair curlers and overpasses,
blue strobes wax and wane between .38 caliber slits
in our louvered doors. The abandoned warehouse
has seventy rooms to be searched.
Each doorjamb wears a caul of daggers.

Cat curls into the booth at Ranch House, lights a cigarette,
lets smoke rings collect on the dresser like loose change.
Blonde waitress leans into your coffee cup,
fresh and steaming among the wingtips.
Cat licks her fingers — the taste lingers
in his nostrils like gas fumes.
She serves seduction with the French fries.
She likes your uniform,
wants it to hang in her closet.
She doesn't hear the sirens.

The Ex

If I were missing,
my ex-husband could find me.
He seeks redemption
and this task would give him penance.
He is best when helping someone
needy and sadly inept.
He wants a stray-cat kind of girl —
with a dog he can bring home,
so I can feed it while I shelter
my own cat, terrified by its snarling.

All those broken locks, those open windows —
he will investigate every one with the stubborn
authority of an ex-cop, searching for that
one true thing, that secret that defines me.

He will cry over all the old photos,
my wedding gown a froth of memory,
new son at my breast — too tender.
And then, relinquish the pain
and find an excuse for an all-night
rendezvous, a compromise, a commingling
with suspect DNA, those crime lab samples
mixed with my old tears,
my lost heartbeat.

Send my ex-husband,
a body memory,
but he says he still loves me,
and if he wins the lottery —
he will pay what he owes.

Bottle Blonde

— CSI Miami

His sunglasses stretching across the Glades,
shading an empathy we mostly believe —
Horatio Caine will fight to gather my DNA,
trace it back to the '60s, when I wandered
thru South Florida, looking for love
in so many places. Find my bottle blonde hair
still floating between the seats of a '65 Ford, tangling
in the fray of cushions, drifting thru the floorboard.

Small clues smile from a yearbook portrait.
An ex-cop, ex-husband makes me easy to trace:
cowering outside the courthouse in a news report,
a ludicrous lawsuit for $1 million,
scrapbook of suppressed desires,
Polaroids hidden in the top drawer,
taped corners, acid paper aging,
inky footprint of my newborn son,

my invisible presence in 1980
at the McDuffie riots:
did Caine sift thru the evidence —
the 3 a.m. seismic fears,
the arrest reports piling high,
blood rust samples
in tiny envelopes —

analyze the ash
that settled into our bedclothes,
dusted our kitchen counter,
fell on our tongues,
and choked us?

Lipstick

— Scott & Bailey

If my car were found abandoned at the airport,
key under the seat, no suitcase in the trunk,
Scott & Bailey would comb their databases,
track down all your lovers and those who witnessed
your betrayals, even my parents, who saw your girlfriend
kiss you goodbye in the hospital after your appendix burst,
after I crouched all night under a blanket
in a surgical waiting room, deserted.

And when they find you, and bring you in
for an interview, they will ask:

> *And if I were to say that your laundry had traces*
> *of a shade of lipstick, not your wife's, what would you say?*
> *And what would you say if I told you we'd found*
> *a long-distance number to Miami on your phone bill,*
> *for 29 minutes at 11:39 p.m., after your wife was asleep?*
> *After you rolled over and said, "Sweet Dreams."*
>
> *Would you deny you made the call?*
> *Would you deny you know her?*
> *If you don't know her, what did you discuss for 29 minutes?*
> *And what will your response be, if we tell you we found a book of poems*
> *dedicated to you and signed, From Gina, in the bookcase?*
> *And what would you say if we told you the phone number*
> *of your midnight call belongs to Gina?*
>
> *And, what would you say if we told you we'd matched*
> *the lipstick on your shirt to a shade on Gina's nightstand?*

After the interview, Janet and Rachel
discuss your half-truths, lies, and denials
while they smoke in the alley, or car park,
and conclude that you have lied,
but not killed me, that I might be on a lark,
an escape, a fling, a proper breakup.

And what if I were to say that
I hurled your *Playboy* magazines
into the front yard, tossed the leash —
the one that belonged to Gina's dog —
moved the bed in front of the window
and painted the bathroom red?

And, if I were to say,
I don't dream about you,
your hands on my thigh —
I don't dream.
What would you say?

Silk

— Megan Russert, Homicide: Life on the Street

She is dressed for a candlelit business lunch,
but leans over a rusty steel desk, a sallow fluorescent
flicker above, crime scene photos and lab reports
combed for that speck of lint, that silk thread
of evidence that leads to the killer's door.

Shoving thru a cluttered hallway,
in heels and linen suit, Kevlar vest pulled
over her shoulder pads like medieval armor,
she kneels next to the victim's head,
while the camera lens discreetly frames
her hands, instead of her hiked-up skirt.

Her silk blouse crushed under her shoulder holster's
leather harness, lustrous thread caught in the buckle, again —
a thread that gnarls and twines along the edge of every seam,
undone under the finest drape of fact and criminal intention.

Accessorized with bus exhaust and masculine
office clatter, she is costumed for irony,
with a soft collar falling open
at the neck. She's surrounded by phones
tattling in the background.
Her sweet-talking interrogation
and tight handcuffs, deliver a conviction.

How she unravels the hem of lies,
how she insists on confession,
how she calls the beast —
growling or coaxing it
from the stench of a dumpster,
how she grips her weapon to fire true,
how she crafts her threadbare need
into steel and cuffs,
and not the rustle of silk.

Four

Serpentine

I hesitate when we embrace in the parking lot, groceries in plastic
bags dangling from both fists, turn my cheek toward your lips.
Your half laugh, your sigh — like hot asphalt, sizzling in the
rain, beginning to fall and chase us to our separate cars.

My other self would risk the kiss, pull you against the cart rack as if I
could transform thunder into desire. My other self would banish
the serpentine memories of regret, fly with you to Ecuador on
my expired passport, ignore the oranges bouncing and rolling
under your truck, the butter softening with each hot kiss.

locked doors,

careful secure safe

burglar
plants a footprint
by the knob
destroys the door
steals jewelry coins
and vacuum cleaner

leaves more
than he takes

Poetics

— Inspector Morse

My empty apartment,
my stale popcorn,
feline screen saver scrolling,
late-night, left-in-a-hurry,
window shattered,
my door-unhinged escape —
and Morse, so sullen
and operatic, assigned to my case.

Above the narrow Oxford streets,
the long and spired day —
nights of foraging
for abandoned books, for chips
and dumpster cuisine, just tossed.

My panic like an alley dog,
a cur — witness
to an unsolved murder,
a crossword crime,
brushstroke in blood,
a golden glimpse —
the killer posed
over the victim,
like Klimt's *Kiss*.

If Morse found me,
I would buy him a pint at the Trout,
argue poetics and Plath
on the bank of the Thames,
Mozart tinting the fog.

Sherlocks

Send all the Sherlocks you know to find me.
Phone New York and London, Japan and Berlin —
empty the flat at 221B Baker Street in every city.
Hundreds of egotistical geniuses will arrive
with their Dr. Watson to assess my case
and search the house for clues.

Deductive reasoning will disparage every speck
of my existence as they squabble
over a motive for abduction, for ransom.
My studio, a mélange of paper and souvenirs,
tangle of cords and cables, my hard drive
sifted for secrets. Dozens of men
in deerstalker hats sit on the porch
smoking calabash pipes and deducing
the likely suspect — each absolutely
sure of his own, and different, conclusion.

Off for the chase, they load in their limousines,
a funereal procession heading away from the house.
The drivers, assaulted with conflicting directions,
slow the cortège to a crawl, then stop for a smoke
while the Watsons convene and discuss an intervention.

It seems like Holmesian deduction would lead
to the same instructions, but the limousines
depart in different directions, circling the town
like drone bees scouting an orchard. At midnight,
they almost collide outside a warehouse floating in fog
along the Thames, sufficiently eerie and threadbare.

Watson pries open a steel door that creaks
and rattles as it reveals a deserted shamble
of crates and empty trunks. Near an open window,
the kidnapper has left a cryptic note
and my monogrammed silver teaspoons,
a cigarette still sputtering on the ledge.

Every Holmes, out the window —
every lantern and flashlight glowing,
searching for tracks and tread marks.
In the end, deduction trumps ego
and the Japanese Sherlock leads the band
to a Bentley, abandoned by the kidnapper
when he became alarmed
at the pursuing hoard of detectives.

Blindfolded and trussed in the trunk —
I have wearied of waiting
for the right Sherlock to come along.

Russian Accent

— *Veronica Mars*

Blonde and smart,
I think she'd find me —
and wage a little class war
along the way. Equipped
with a Russian accent
when she needs it,
a telephoto lens and reams
of smart dialogue, she is
the opposite of the dream
I have about going
back to high school,
and failing my last class —
scrambling, incompetent,
late, and clueless again —
after 40 years of
successful adulthood.

Her wisecracks, crisp and funny,
her pranks, the perfect payback.
But her love life is as baffling
as my high school skirmishes
with passion — all innuendo
and confusion, silences
that languish in hallways,
door jambs supporting
lovesick boys, moments of glee
and hours of unrelieved boredom.
Anticipation like a drug,
and then the perfect kiss,
the one to remember,
or imagine.

High Stakes

— Maverick

When I am stranded and broke in a western town
with a hapless name like Oblivion or Apocalypse,
send Bret Maverick to rescue me.

When he ambles thru the swinging doors
of the Palace Saloon and heads
for an open game, it's jacks or better,
spades flush, inside straights,
red diamonds, a bluff and a kicker,
but never penny ante.

Black hat tilted back — a rogue, a con,
but no marked decks, no aces
palmed, no double dealing or fistfights,
no manual labor, no whiskey or champagne,
just anti-heroic grins and a bad aim —
and when he saddles up and rides
into a black and white sunset,
he leaves behind girls like me —

still stretched out in the living room,
watching on Sunday night —
awakening to the dealings of the heart,
the odds and shuffling, the higher stakes.

Passport Expired

— Chasing Shadows

I have become snapshots on his white board,
a pile of phone records and texts, credit ratings
and bank statements, forming a pattern
of essentially boring forensics —
to Sean Stone, I am a magic marker web
of simplicity, my movements uncomplicated
until I fade from the landscape
into the unkempt trees on High Road,
or the maze of interchanges at I-10,
my black-and-white-video ghost
kissing the yellow line on the off-ramp.

During interviews, interrogations,
hallway conversations, he is intent,
and listening, until he is not,
and walks away — no coffee shop
conversations, no filler dialogue, just paper
records stacked and thumbed,
just tap tap tap — keyboard on fire.

His Google search reveals:
my book is valued at 152 dollars
or maybe 47 cents;
that I may have been killed
and profiled on NBC's *Dateline*,
and dated Nick on *The Playboy Club*,
that I have appeared in scattered
bookish locations around the world,
at least digitally, as my passport
expired unused. By page six,
his search shifts from mistaken identities

into meaningless keyword jumbles,
with offers to find me *for a fee*.

Disappointed that I am so habitual that cats
congregate at my door every morning —
but, he discovers I used to kiss like a storm cloud
heavy with rain, unpredictable lightning strikes,
a delicate roll of thunder, until I fell
into a swimming pool in South Dade,
feeling slightly pornographic
instead of erotic —
lost in the chlorine
and a subtropical sauna
of exposed flesh.

And, six weeks later,
fell into a wedding dress,
and a marriage —
an epic of habit,
with a shelf for every passion,
a jar for every angry word,
until betrayal replaced ritual,
until keening conformed
to a hollow and perfect silence.

Just One More Thing

— Columbo (for Al)

His offhand questions
and rumpled raincoat,
his glance of one eye —
as if all thought has rolled to the right,
and light could enter at a left-handed slant —
as if an angel has been lurking.

But that is later, when *Wings of Desire*
dip earthward on film, and Columbo
is revealed as a former angel
who explains the habits of the corporeal.
His raincoat hiding scars from severed wings,
he has chosen the coffee
and the pears, the human shiver
and caress, over listening
forever to our stray conversations,

He will find every clue,
whether it leads past
summer's late hydrangeas,
now faded and papery wafers
of sunlight, or random fingerprints
from the pen left on my nightstand.

Just one more thing
ringed in cigar smoke,
just one more thing
to reveal the missing clue,
the feather of truth
that falls to earth.

Rift

— River

In the hollow of a distant field,
in the boat of my redemption,
or a rift in the road
that rends an afterlife —
I confront John River.
Costumed in time's delicate silk,
I roam an ambivalent space between breath
and transformation. He is alarmed by me,
still confounded by his new ability
to interrogate the dead.

I found him before the cosmic unraveling,
that last transformation that leaves behind
only my wishes to be read aloud —
my will that I had left undone until I imagined
my son, adrift in the house where he grew up,

still so torn about his destination —
not knowing there is no place
to conveniently arrive,
that there is always more,
until there isn't.

Cleaved by time's arrow,
I could become only distance
in the equation, a whiff of garlic,
fluorescent hum, trace
of blood illuminated,
a detective's footnote.

Let John River make an arrest
before my elevator doors
close — before my haunting.

Prom King

— Beau Felton, Homicide: Life on the Street

In high school, he is the guy with friends
and girlfriends, letter jackets,
and twenty pictures in the yearbook,
his smile in focus, his rakish hair
and sleepy eyes. His high hopes
for a life of homecoming glory
with endless parades and parties lost
with mediocre grades — earned for him
by earnest girls with dreamy crushes, girls
he repays with nonchalant kisses outside his locker
as he slips their pages into his empty notebook.

Now, he is murder police — charming informants,
drinking free coffee, smoking borrowed cigarettes,
carelessly tossing a battered football in the squad room,
his desk an unkempt wasteland of empty mugs
and bobbleheads, unfiled papers in lazy heaps.
His red-headed partner, an earnest woman
with perfection on her mind, finishes his reports.
His strategy is sometimes a subtle flirtation,
a grin that still inspires trust, and a physical power
leftover from high school football drills,
but now drifting away in a sea of boozy plastic cups.

How he loves to break down doors
or slam them shut with that metallic riff
of steel striking steel, how he regrets
the lost lullaby of his children,
their cherubic faces shadowed
in a nightlight glow, his wife
asleep in their half-lit bedroom —

how he rues that last stumble
toward his bed at 3 a.m., whiskey and sex
masked with mouthwash.
How he searches the empty rooms
for evidence when she leaves —
how the house chokes and rattles,
how dreams slip away.

False Kiss

— *The Sopranos*

If I go missing, don't send Tony Soprano to find me.
He might tell you there was a misunderstanding,
a moral quandary, a Secaucus swamp
of the intellect, a swift kick from
the unexamined life, suddenly examined.

Danger's embrace might have been thrilling,
but you could find me trussed in his basement,
alone with a kaleidoscope of bruised and fractured
toes, a swirling prism of small pink fingernails.

He could exchange his gift of a diamond necklace
for a cement choker, my shaking hands
mortared together, clutching a prayer.

Who can breathe when affection
is such a tenuous kiss,
a missed cheek, a glance
over the shoulder into the camera,
a gesture that foreshadows suffocation,
an exposed throat.

Forget his false kiss —
a dream snake
slithering in the foyer.

Whitewashed

— *after Rectify*

At first it is a sickening thing. To feel seems like having a disease.
But you get used to sensations over time.

— Louise Erdrich, LaRose

Talk founders amid a sense
      of chains, jolt of steel doors slid shut,
a stutter mid-sentence, words tremor, evade the throat
      as despair paints its prison on the wall,
      the bars, the light, its false fluorescence
      in a quiet cell.

And then, an open field — a colossus
of wind, its lumbering footsteps
prowling in the underbrush.
      Still, the bars throw themselves
      across the road, grapple with the yellow line,
      twine around the steering wheel.

The green swale, even in winter
      disconcerting, the scattered stones —
      like whitewashed skulls still incarcerated —
a breath caught, shoulders quake, recalling
      the first cuff, first leg iron,
      their mandated shuffle.

False confessions echo in teenage anthems,
      a shoebox soundtrack of drive-ins,
      carhop pizza, and voices
      from the backseat singing off-key.

Even in dreams,
       mouth taped shut — visitors clouded in a glass partition,
       muffled voices from the phone on the other side of the wall.

Starting over with a small duffel bag
       of expectations, there is a longing
       fulfilled by the ocean, by submersion,
       and lobster dinners,
       by driving the same
       lost highway.

Five

Jay Feathers

Leaving inadvertent evidence of my existence — less intentional
than blue jay feathers from the driveway saved in an envelope,
more like coffee spills or greasy pans, a forgotten black shawl
draped over the back of a restaurant chair.

Unvoiced gratitude, lost embraces, my small cruelties — gossip,
snark, or slight — abandoned. A chain of tainted evidence, my
DNA — clinging to my toothbrush, sloughed on my bedclothes,
my shoes — is invisible, trampled, traveling without me.

Detectives rifling and ransacking my house could excavate secrets
pushed to the back of my closet — a surgical boot, opioids, love
notes: a history of my traumas.

each letter broken

as if ascenders kept toppling
while the round sure breasts
of the "B" suddenly rupture
flattened like an old tire
and the tails twitch frantically
dragging along the next line
deflating
punctuating
hen scratched
cursively
entrapped
between the faint blue lines
of an old composition book

words compromise
language cripples
unstrung
aphasia
slipping
into diction
misunderstanding
scrawling like
a virus

broken
like a heart
no
words

Subterranean

— NYPD Blue

If you lose me in New York City,
send Bobby Simone to find me —
his sunglasses reflect a generous heart.
Imagine me in that opening TV teaser,
walking across the same New York street —
my own shades sizzling with that sexy aura.

Look for me in Manhattan, stylish on Fifth Avenue,
or schlepping in the Bronx. Take a ferry to Staten Island.
Let the Hudson lift into your face, that beautiful face.
Investigate my mother's old apartment in Brooklyn,
where Uncle George made bathtub gin. Look up
my college roommate in Queens.

It is the city cleft in our imagination,
a familiar landscape, binding our dreams of fame
with nightmares of falling, with ash
ghosting bodies as they leap from the towers.

In New York City, the subway swallows dreams —
its subterranean mysteries tunnel under the East River,
the chug-chunk-clang beating a rhythm, seductive,
crime on Fifth Avenue, a theatrical redemption staged
in front of St. Patrick's Cathedral, the mercies.

In Gramercy Park, search my grandmother's brownstone
or cross the bridge and find my cousin in Jersey.
Amble thru the Cloisters, and trace my parking ticket
from their overcrowded lot, recall my story about the frenzied
horde of teenage girls searching for the Beatles
outside the Museum of Modern Art.

Track down my imaginary apartment in the Village,
the paint-smeared diction of our parallel life,
find the doppelgänger who stole my palette knife,
my typewriter, your lost souvenirs at the Port Authority,
my poems abandoned at the Cornelia Street Café,
ruined stockings in Rockefeller Plaza, my shoes
washed up in Jamaica Bay, find everything —
that trace of joy we left, strolling in the city.

Alpine

— The Girl with the Dragon Tattoo

The girl with the dragon tattoo
is almost dozing, black mascara
staining her cheeks as she watches
surveillance video, and rewinds
your rain-soaked kidnapping.
Lisbeth knows your binary code, your pixels
floating on her screen, finds our messages
pirouetting into the ether. At last, she identifies
the mountains, blurred in black and white,
behind your mouth taped shut.

You are a smeared silhouette struggling on the screen,
surveilled with GPS and heat-seeking drones.
Evidence of your flesh and confinement
stacks up in Chinese servers, pings thru Denmark,
a credit-card trail picked up in the Alps,
skip-traced from a burner phone
to a black van on a switchback,
fishtailing in the rain, grazing the guardrail —
barely avoiding a 10,000-foot plunge into the valley.

Lisbeth is leading the search
to find you. Her unforgiving fists
and networked fingers track the gang
in the rusted black van across western peaks,
and into a warehouse south of Stockholm,
where a hulking leather-clad fascist
has bound you with duct tape and chains.

Your ransom is ridiculous, but Lisbeth
brings you home. Her stealth defeating
phantoms, finding that hollow house of the mind
that steals clocks, and stalls the universe —
like seven minutes of goodbye, obscured by mist
on the window of our train, slowly departing.

Sensible Shoes

— *Vera*

Tromping thru the moors,
adroit intellect hidden beneath
a dowdy knit cloche —
Vera Stanhope is a practical woman,
most happy investigating murder.

Vera inspires my shopping sprees —
watching her trudge the docks in ill-fitting tweed,
sharp eyes memorizing the crime scene,
plodding thru dingy factories,
or the spiny gorse in a meadow,
always in sensible shoes,
so brusquely brown —
I vowed to die in elegant clothes.

If she opens my closet door, an avalanche
of shoes — red, aqua, navy, brown, pink,
and black patent leather — would land at her feet.
Forgive my shallow love of flowing silk
and Mary Jane shoes — a pretension, a denial
of aging, flesh camouflaged beneath a flounce
of color or maybe leopard skin.

Sift thru the jumble of earrings
left on my dresser and find the pair
that's incomplete, that dangles
without its mate — an elusive clue to motive.

Steel Spurs

— Justified

Raylan Givens has a cowboy hat!
And, that saddles my twelve-year-old self
on the silver palomino of imagination.
I become a heroine who rides like a boy,
wears dusty chaps and tarnished steel spurs.

If I lean on the rail at the High Note Bar,
dusted, parched from a long day's drive,
his laconic drawl, like Kentucky bluegrass
soughing in the holler, charms me
with a bourbon and suddenly,
it would seem worth it to be a girl.

When he feels *justified,*
men slump forward on their sofas,
fall backward into the river,
dive too late over the porch rail.
All shot, all buried with some regret.

Loving women like a comet, all hot and fiery —
he is not the constant star you might prefer,
but perfect in the moment he lights your sky.

If I were lost, he would search the hills
of Harlan County, park his truck near
the likeliest creek bed, bust barbed wire
and hillbillies to bring me home.

Later, just to ensure I am no longer at risk,
he will visit, infrequently.

.

Witness

— Frank Pembleton, Homicide: Life on the Street

The confusions of
thunder breaking
and lightning bounding over
the harbor at Fels Point.

The only witness, a bird, escaped
from its cage and dropping
feathers into the crime scene.

Look up, Frank, and find the song of reckoning
falling from the dented roof, sifting in the cobwebs,
a gauzy aria of your Jesuit doubt.

He is ambivalent, in the squad car, musing
about god's intemperance — a loss of faith taunting
the most faithful of investigators.

His interrogation style so close, he suffocates
the suspect. In *the box,* he pulls at secrets
like existential taffy, matches the murderer's unease
with a searing grin — white teeth, fierce eyes, full screen.

Thru the one-way mirror at the station,
the bird watches Frank pace, hover,
inject discomfort into each glance and mimic.
Silent witness, bird banging wings against the glass,
bulleting its beak, almost breaking the mirror.

Its voice, only a trill —
not words, but lament,
not speech, but omen.

Abandoned Car Park

— Braquo

Don't send Eddy Caplan and his sad-eyed gang
of Robin Hoods to find me.
They have crossed the yellow line —
their sense of law, like rough gravel
lost in a gutter on the Rue de Bonaparte.

In their attempted rescues,
I am more likely to be buried alive
or ticking off my last minute
in an abandoned car park,
staring down at a suicide vest.

If I examine that moment,
its tiny flakes of forethought
littering the empty garage,
a clock's ravaged hands
merciless and ticking
above the greasy floor,
there is no future, only now —
just sixty seconds before the explosion.
Only ticking. Only now.

No more cat purr or lingering breakfasts on the porch
no laced embraces — your hands, your hands,
no transatlantic flights, or penthouse dinners.

For pleasures soon lost — a farewell,
launching our hearts into the stratosphere,
32 miles from yesterday, gasping.

A Melancholy Intellect

— Cracker

There is a melancholy in intellect,
in the fierce tools of a mind set loose
in lesser mental terrain, a terror of dissection.

Fitz ferrets out the fragile neurons, plucks
from them, our lies. They fall on the table
to be sorted and tagged or left to thrash
as he watches — as if extracting fact
were an elegant torture, a curious blaze,
a rational rape of the soul.

He is, without smoke and booze, bets and sex,
lost in his own house — a rumpled psychologist
reeking of nicotine — too alien,
and wrecked, too shambling, and late.

If you consent to an interview with him,
he will rive and rend all that shapes you,
barter your tender sanity for what is secret
between us. Each revelation — a trust, broken.

Underground

— *Prime Suspect*

Disappeared in London — last seen slipping
down the stairwell at Monument Station,
fleeing ennui, that boring suitor.

    In the incident room for my disappearance,
    Jane Tennison gathers herself to confront her churlish
    male team — their thwarts swallowed like whiskey
    burning the throat, then shrewdly quelled
    with instinct, with rank, and will.

Stepping off a platform in the Tube,
memories of Paris smudge the glass,
ignite like sparks from the rails,
from the car's tremor and rock.

    Escaped to the stairwell to smoke,
    to think, and sort her evidence —
    proof of my existence trapped in
    a sliding door, a twist of scarf, a last glimpse.

Aroused from Underground slumber,
and exiting the car, sleek doors almost embrace me,
steel lover, thief of my heart, Parisian lullaby.

    Jane, a prioress of fleeting lovers, who place mostly
    second to ambition mixed with vodka and tonic —
    her frustrations always sporting trousers
    and a loosened Windsor knot.

Find me in Paris — after wine
at a small café, torn baguette,
a little cheese, *pension* on the Left Bank,
a love to last the night.

Juxtaposition of the Mermaid

— after Homicide: Life on the Street

Pembleton and Bayliss
will discuss the meaning of my life
and I will finally know the answer
with a lapsed Catholic, Buddhist slant.

In Baltimore, where the dirty snow piles up
around the harbor, the plows come out
at 5 a.m. and push late-night promises
to the curb along with slushy trash.
I left a trail of syllables and scarves,
lost my boots in Fells Point —
feral and vanished,
24 hours of searching.

Bayliss will wonder about the two ugly Hotai in my studio
(made by my mother and banned
as pagan religious objects by my father).
Pembleton will question the juxtaposition of the mermaid,
and the flamingo with luscious red and yellow peppers,
the photo of Uma Thurman as June Miller,
and Maria de Medeiros as Anaïs Nin,
all eyes and smoky sex. There is something secret
to uncover, old love letters —
little gasps in the nightstand.

Frank and Tim will sit on the porch
parsing my life, looking for a thread to
unravel my disappearance, my suspect origins.

Have I died here, watching the harbor,
disappeared in the shoals?
No autopsy, no reason,
so *Sartre* in my demise.
As Frank and Tim reconstruct my life,
I am stricken with its small squalors,
the lost teeth of dreams, the disordered closet,
the ransacked stacks of paper,
evidence piled high for an anti-climax,
an accounting so baffling that
being found alive would only embarrass.
I must oblige the script,
its need for dénouement,
for dying.

Epilogue

Eclipse

A perfect apex of morning light falling across the kitchen table before the eaves eclipse the sun.

I could sculpt a room with light saved from this morning, a slice of shadow from the pines across the road that block the rays until mid-morning. I would sketch the eaves like a hat, allowing the sun to lie at the precise angle required to encase silence. Blown glass would balance a sphere of light within a cube of flux and fire. I would murmur into the sphere and it would roll in a meditation, not quite prayer, but mindful of its shape.

I would fashion light and hold it fast, defy its speed and transience. Call it home. Call it tamed.

broken at the cortex

a stem swaying
in the wind
now untethered
untended

hot air suspires
kite becomes
sparrow

Just Rising

If I go missing,
there will be no drama,
no broken wings,
no cancer splayed
across my chest,
no heart poised to leap
and pray for forgiveness.

No, and no.
No tears falling
like a madonna
miracle of September,
no candles setting
the curtains ablaze.

No terrors spiking midnight,
no skin scarred and pierced,
no black tattoos triangulating
desperation with hope,
no brown leaves suddenly
falling, no falling,
no gravity.

Just rising.
Just fierce opposition.
Just morning light
falling across the table,
blessing every plate.

And sorrow.
Just a mouth of blue sky.
Just light.
Just cat tongue
licking my cheek
on waking.
Just coffee, still hot.
Just air,
warm and stirring.
Just wren song.

Notes

After watching an episode of the Swedish detective series, *Wallander*, I thought, "If I go missing, I want Kurt Wallander to find me." That was the impetus for the first poem written in the series. His careful observation and respect for the objects in the house of the missing person were a touching contrast to his careless personal life. This metaphor of search opened a new way to explore loss, memory, exposure, and regret. These notes are offered as some context for the poems in the *If I Go Missing* series.

Braquo (page 76)

> Setting: Hautes-de-Seine area of Paris; the DPDJ, the criminal investigation division of the Police Nationale; contemporary
>
> Characters/Actors: four police agents — Eddy Caplan (Jean-Hugues Anglade), Walter Morlighem (Joseph Malerba), Théo Vachewski (Nicolas Duvauchelle), and Roxanne Delgado (Karole Rocher)
>
> Air date: 2009–2016

The Bridge / Broen / Bron (page 23)

> Setting: title refers to the Øresund Bridge connecting Copenhagen, Denmark with Malmö, Sweden; contemporary
>
> Character/Actors: Swedish police Detective Saga Norén (Sofia Helin), who is neurodivergent, and her Danish counterpart, Detective Martin Rohde (Kim Bodnia)
>
> Original Air: 2011–2018

Chasing Shadows (page 58)

Setting: a Missing Persons Field Unit in London; contemporary

Character/Actors: DS Sean Stone (Reece Shearsmith), a former homicide investigator now analyst, and Ruth Hattersley (Alex Kingston)

Original Air: 2014

Columbo (page 60)

Setting: Los Angeles Police Department; contemporary

Character/Actors: Italian-American Homicide Detective Frank Columbo (Peter Falk)

Original Air: 1968–2003

Cracker (page 77)

Setting: Manchester, England; contemporary

Character/Actors: criminal psychologist Dr. Edward "Fitz" Fitzgerald (Robbie Coltrane), works with the Greater Manchester Police to help them solve crimes and DS Jane Penhaligon (Geraldine Somerville)

Original Air: 1993–1996

CSI Miami (page 45)

Setting: Miami, Florida; contemporary

Character/Actors: Lt. Horatio Caine (David Caruso), a detective assigned to the Miami-Dade Police Department's Crime Scene Investigation Unit

Original Air: 2002–2012

The Girl with the Dragon Tattoo (page 71)

> Setting: Stockholm, Sweden; 2002
>
> Character/Actors: Lisbeth Salander (Noomi Rapace), a
> brilliant surveillance agent and hacker and Mikael
> Blomkvist (Michael Nyqvist), publisher of *Millennium*
> magazine
>
> Original Air: 2009, Swedish film based on the novels of Stieg
> Larsson

Homicide: Life on the Street (pages 48, 62, 75, 79)

> Setting: Baltimore Homicide Squad; contemporary
>
> Characters/Actors: Beau Felton (Daniel Baldwin), Frank
> Pembleton (Andre Braugher), Meldrick Lewis (Clark
> Johnson), Kay Howard (Melissa Leo), Tim Bayliss (Kyle
> Secor), Megan Russert (Isabella Hofmann)
>
> Original Air: 1993–1999

Inspector Morse (page 53)

> Setting: Oxford, England; contemporary
>
> Character/Actors: Endeavor Morse (John Thaw), Detective
> Chief Inspector with the Thames Valley Police force, and
> Sergeant Robert "Robbie" Lewis (Kevin Whately)
>
> Original Air: 1987–2000

Justified (page 74)

> Setting: Lexington, Kentucky and in the Appalachian
> Mountains of eastern Kentucky, in and around Harlan
> County; contemporary
>
> Character/Actors: Raylan Givens (Timothy Olyphant), a
> U.S. Marshal, and Boyd Crowder (Walton Goggins), a
> local criminal and Givens' boyhood friend
>
> Original Air: 2010–2015

Life (page 17)

Setting: Los Angeles; contemporary

Character/Actors: Charlie Crews (Damien Lewis), a Los Angeles Police Department detective released from prison after serving twelve years for a murder he did not commit, and his partner, Detective Dani Reese (Sarah Shahi)

Original Air: 2007–2009

Luther (page 19)

Setting: London; contemporary

Character/Actors: Detective Chief Inspector John Luther (Idris Elba), Metropolitan Police Service, Serious Crime Unit, and Alice Morgan (Ruth Wilson), a research scientist, genius-IQ psychopath, and murder suspect

Original Air: 2010–2019

Maverick (page 57}

Setting: American Old West; 1870s

Character/Actors: Bret Maverick (James Garner), an adroitly articulate cardsharp, his brother Bart (Jack Kelly), his cousin Beau (Roger Moore)

Original Air: 1957–1962

NYPD Blue (page 69)

Setting: fictional 15th Precinct of New York City Police Department; contemporary

Character/Actors: Detective Bobby Simone (Jimmy Smits), and Detective Andy Sipowicz (Dennis Franz)

Original Air: 1993–2005

Prime Suspect (page 78)

Setting: London; contemporary

Character/Actors: Jane Tennison (Helen Mirren), one of
the first female Detective Chief Inspectors in Greater
London's Metropolitan Police Service

Original Air: 1991–2006

Rectify (page 65)

Setting: Paulie, Georgia; contemporary

Character/Actors: Daniel Holden (Aden Young), released from
prison after 20 years thru the discovery of conflicting
DNA evidence, and Amantha Holden (Abigail Spencer),
Daniel's younger sister

Original Air: 2013–2016

River (page 61)

Setting: London; contemporary

Character/Actors: Detective Inspector John River (Stellan
Skarsgård), Metropolitan Police Service, and DS
Jackie "Stevie" Stevenson (Nicola Walker), his recently
murdered colleague

Original Air: 2015

Scott & Bailey (page 46)

Setting: Manchester England; contemporary

Characters/Actors: Detective Constable Janet Scott (Lesley
Sharp) and Detective Constable Rachel Bailey (Suranne
Jones), members of the Major Incident Team of the
fictional Manchester Metropolitan Police

Original Air: 2011–2016

Sherlock Holmes (page 54)

Setting: London, New York, Japan

Character/Actors: Sherlock Holmes, the most portrayed literary character in film and television history, has appeared on screen almost 500 times as of 2021. The list of actors who play Holmes and his confidant, Dr. Watson, is almost as long.

Original Air (stage, film, television): 1899–present

The Sopranos (page 64)

Setting: northern New Jersey; contemporary

Character/Actors: New Jersey-based Italian-American mobster Tony Soprano (James Gandolfini), his wife Carmela (Edie Falco), and psychiatrist Jennifer Melfi (Lorraine Bracco)

Original Air: 1999–2007

True Detective, Season 1 (page 21)

Setting: Southern Louisiana; 1995–2012

Character/Actors: Louisiana State Police homicide detectives Marty Hart (Woody Harrelson) and Rust Cohle (Matthew McConaughey)

Original Air: 2014

Vera (page 73)

Setting: Northumberland, England; contemporary

Character/Actors: Detective Chief Inspector Vera Stanhope (Brenda Blethin) of the fictional Northumberland & City Police

Original Air: 2011–present

Veronica Mars (page 56)

Setting: fictional seaside town of Neptune, California; contemporary

Character/Actors: high school reporter and private detective, Veronica Mars (Kristen Bell), and her father, sheriff/private detective Keith Mars (Enrico Colantoni)

Original Air: 2004–2007 (Seasons 1–3), 2014 (movie), 2019 (Season 4)

Wallander (page 13)

Setting: Ystad, Sweden; contemporary

Character/Actors: homicide detective Kurt Wallander (Krister Henriksson)

Original Air: 2005–2014 (Swedish television)

Title Index

First Line Index

About the Author

Carol Lynne Knight is the co-director of Anhinga Press, where she designs covers and text, and edits books. She is the author of three books of poetry, *If I Go Missing* (Fernwood Press, 2022), *A Fretted Terrain, Like Mars* (Apalachee Press, 2020), and *Quantum Entanglement* (Apalachee Press, 2010). She is the co-editor of *Snakebird: Thirty Years of Anhinga Poets*.

Her poetry has appeared in *Another Chicago Magazine*, *Louisiana Literature*, *Tar River Review*, *Poetry Motel*, *Earth's Daughters*, *The Ledge*, *Slipstream*, *Broome Review*, *J*, *Comstock Review*, *Northwest Florida Review*, *Epicenter*, *Redactions*, *Iconoclast*, *Epicenter*, *HazMat*, *So to Speak*, *Down in the Dirt Magazine*, *Cagibi*, *Rivet*, *Slink Chunk*. and in the anthologies *Off the Cuffs* (Soft Skull Press), *Touched by Eros* (Live Poets Society), *The Poets Guide to the Birds* (Anhinga Press), *Beloved on the Earth* (Holy Cow! Press), and *North of Wakulla* (Anhinga Press).

Born in Michigan, she grew up in South Florida and graduated from the University of Miami and Florida State University with degrees in Art Education. She has exhibited her drawings, pottery, sculpture, and digital images in the eastern U.S. In other lives, she has worked as an art teacher, potter, videographer, and graphic designer. She lives in Tallahassee, Florida.

CPSIA information can be obtained
at www.ICGtesting.com
Printed in the USA
BVHW032115010522
635412BV00005B/19